Poetry for the Soul

Robin J.

Dedicated to my Beautiful Kids –
Shevonta, Blake, Larrielle, Larry III, LaRon, and
D'Anthony, my Granddaughter Payton Kim Marie,
my Dad (Eddie), Mom (Mary) and my Ma T (Theresa)
You are all my reasons why!

Poetry for the Soul

Poetry doesn't have to be so complex
Using big words to sound clever
Stretching our minds beyond our own consciousness
Using metaphors and twisting our words to mean so much more
Stroking our ink onto paper
Hoping it touches someone's soul
Hoping someone, anyone, feels it in their heart,
in their spirit
Poetry doesn't have to be so complex
Expressing our most inner thoughts
Our deepest feelings
All our jubilations and afflictions
and everything life brings us in between
Subliminally throwing things out in the universe with our wordplay
Hoping someone grasp the meaning
Praying it all sinks in and touches one person's soul
And when we're finished pouring our words out
For all the world to hear
Snapping fingers, smiling faces, and applause are all we want in the end
Poetry can be as easy as 1, 2, 3 and ABC's
No matter how deeply or easily we choose to articulate our words
In the end
We just want someone, anyone, to get the meaning

Robin J.

Poetry

"Literary work in which special intensity is given to the expression of feelings and ideas by the use of distinctive style and rhythm; poems collectively or as a genre of literature."

Soul

"Emotional or intellectual energy or intensity, especially as revealed in a work of art or an artistic performance."

A POET

Embeds their secrets in their ink
Tucking them in rhymes and lines
Each verse exposing their truths
Anticipating the moment
You find them

Robin J.

All I want is to vocalize all these words
Trapped in my head
The words just get caught up in my throat
How sad that I cannot articulate the words that I wrote
I wanna go hard, give it my all, be cutthroat
The words just won't come out; I feel like I'm about to choke

I'm sweating; my mind is trying hard to think steady
Nerves rattlin' *Please, Lord, let there be no distractions*
I wanna share my words so the crowd has satisfaction
I'm losing my focus, mind racing
Thinking about. . .tragic thoughts, happy thoughts, crazy thoughts
All the words swirling around in my head
Thinking of everything but the words that need to be said

They get stuck; the words get lost in my chaotic mind
And my rhymes seem to have gotten lost in time
Damn! I just want to articulate the words that I wrote
But the words won't flow out, feeling like I'm about to choke

What do I need to do to unlock these words inside of me
These words I wrote, stroke for stroke
Just open my mouth and speak; it seems so damn easy
Crazy that my constant thinking is getting the best of me
Making this harder than I know it has to be

If I could only let the words flow out
What if I forget a line, get it all wrong
My timing and my rhymes
I am scared they will come out all wrong
The words, they get lost from the glares of the stares
Oh no! I feel like I'm about to choke!

Breathe...I just want to articulate the words that I wrote!
Lord, please forgive me of my sins
And allow these words to flow out of me
Let this stage fright end and my words take flight
Let me just articulate the words that I wrote

WRITE A HAIKU POEM

A haiku poem is composed of only 3 lines. The first line of the haiku has 5 syllables, the second line has 7 syllables, and the third has 5 syllables.

Example:
In the midst of life
I learned what it truly means
To love life again

Your turn. Write a haiku poem of your own...

_____

_____

_____

_____

_____

_____

_____

_____

_____

_____

Robin J.

When all those pieces of yesterday
Come back in one full sweep
You cannot hide from them
You cannot run from them
Even though you have suppressed them for years
When those pieces catch up with you
There is no controlling it
There is no holding it all in
You must let it flow out
Like a waterfall pounding the rocks below
Allow them to plunge to the bottom and smoothly flow
downstream
And just. . .Let all that Sh@t go!

ONE WORD...

Sometimes, ONE WORD can
Sum up everything you are feeling
Sometimes, a complete sentence
Is not necessary
To reach into the depths of someone's soul

Robin J.

WORD PROMPT!

Quibble . . . *to argue or complain about small, unimportant things*

He always liked to **quibble** whenever I tried to rest
Constantly putting our love to the test
Laying with the pillow over my head
Constantly making me wonder
If this relationship is what is best

Your turn. Use the word *quibble* to create a poem…

_____

_____

_____

_____

_____

_____

_____

_____

_____

_____

_____

O' Romeo, Romeo
Where art thou Romeo!!
You came and swept me off my feet
Unexpectedly, like a thief
Brought love and light into my life
My soul I bared to you
I trust you would do it no harm
Never did you use my sins against me
You embraced me in your loving arms
Your heart you entrusted me with
I keep it locked away
Protected always with my life
Just know I am here to stay
Our lives forever intertwined
Our minds as one
Our souls intermixed
My love you have won
Enthralled with the thought of you
Of us
And how MASTERFULLY this love is

Robin J.

He wanted something
I could not give

Something I never knew how
Or desired ever to acquire

He wanted my love
To show me what it wasn't

He wanted my heart
To break into tiny pieces

He wanted my soul
So I would be broken forever

He wanted me to trust him
So I would never trust again

He wanted me whole
So I would have nothing left
To give

Sometimes you just need to. . .
Pull back from certain People, Places, Things, Situations,
Feelings and Life
And just BE

With
Absolutely
Nobody around
Drown out all the chatter

And just BE
Yourself
Alone
To gather your thoughts
To find your peace
To get to know yourself all over again, separate from life
For a moment
So you can love on yourself unapologetically with no
distractions

All alone in all your nakedness
And allow yourself to be totally
Forthright,
Truthful,
Unobstructed and Loyal
If but for a moment to YOURSELF for YOURSELF

Those that genuinely care. . .won't mind

Robin J.

You will
Be too much
For some people

Some people cannot
Take YOU at 100% YOU
And that is okay
Those are NOT
The people for you

SMILE
And move on out of their way

WRITE AN ACROSTIC POEM

A poem in which the first letter of each line spells out a word, name, or phrase when read vertically.

Living each day
One day at a time
Vivid rays of sunshine peer through
Each day is a blessing to feel love and be loved

Your turn. Write an acrostic poem of your own...

_____

_____

_____

_____

_____

_____

_____

_____

_____

_____

_____

Robin J.

I don't want to point blame
But. . .
Maybe, just maybe
We are two f@cked-up people who don't know how to love
genuinely
Or how to allow anyone to truly love us.
And maybe
We don't know how to put our own bullsh@t aside to even
attempt to be able to genuinely love or allow ourselves to be
loved.

At night, when I am
Lying awake in bed
Looking up at the ceiling
Lost in thought…

I do not think of you!
And I laugh to myself

Robin J.

S H E

"I believe that people can change. I believe that some people truly learn from their past. That they can move beyond it and be anew."

~ Robin. J

SHE is not that same girl you once knew
Who only thought
About
Herself
Who did not know how to love
Or how
to be LOVED

SHE is no longer
That hurt little girl
Who could not let go of all the pain
That caused her to play games with men's hearts
Discarding them like a used paper towel
And always staying one step ahead
Protecting her own heart
Only ever considering herself
Because it felt better that way

SHE who fell into the abyss
Of
Heartbreaks, mistakes, casual sex, and loneliness
That caused her heart to grow cold

SHE has moved past her
SHE no longer exists
Life has changed her
In ways only God knows
SHE has emerged this
Beautiful soul
Moving past lost loves
Healing from past pain
Believing in the passion
Of connecting
With someone so deeply
That the two become one
Believing in love

SHE has
Learned
How to love
And what love truly is
No longer living selfishly
SHE is ready to give
Ready for love
And to be loved
SHE is not the same girl she once was

Robin J.

SHE now knows her worth
SHE is now a woman of growth
Progression
Adaptation
Revision
Evolution
SHE is. . .A Woman of New

Like a Dandelion
She felt "PRETTY"
But she knew she was not
Ever anyone's favorite
Never picked to be in a bouquet
Never picked to be in a corsage
Never picked to be in anything
Except by that small child
On a warm sunny day
Playing in the yard
Who picked her for their mother
Who thought she was the
Most beautiful flower ever

Robin J.

My secrets I keep locked away
No one knows my pain
Or sees my shame
I would never give them
Satisfaction of knowing my life pains
All I allow them to see
Is the exterior of me, the "I am okay" me
Not the deep interior of me, the broken me
Knowing they would only try and use it against me
Every secret tucked deep
In the depths of my past
Locked away, and only I have the key
As I sway past, I feel the people's stares
Their unapproving glares
The sun, I swear, has lost its gleam
The winds blow hard
As if trying to blow all my secrets from me
The trees murmur my name
As leaves whispered, *Tell me your shame*
All wanting to know my secrets
I bet now
You want to know
My secrets, too!

WRITE A HAIKU POEM USING THE WORD "EXPRESSION"

A haiku poem is composed of only 3 lines. The first line of the haiku has 5 syllables, the second line has 7 syllables, and the third has 5 syllables.

My *expression* showed
I did not have to explain
My face said it all

Your turn. Write a haiku poem of your own...

_____

_____

_____

_____

_____

_____

_____

_____

Robin J.

When you love someone
Sometimes you give up your whole soul
You give up every ounce of your being
Just to be with that person

You lose yourself
In them
In their world
Their days become your days
Their friends become your friends
Their family, your family

You let go of so much of your life, of yourself
You get lost in the layers
Of their world

To only find out later
When it ends
You do not know who you are
What you like, what you love

Now
Your left
Picking up the pieces, trying to heal the scars
Trying to figure it all out
Who you are, what you like, what's your life
Where do you go from here
What is the plan, and how do you begin again

28

When you love someone
Sometimes you lose yourself along the way
Sometimes you find yourself
And sometimes
You just pick up the pieces
And pray you will be okay

Robin J.

Joy comes in the morning, so they say
Joy comes to me in many different ways
Joy comes to me in watching my kids grow
Joy comes in watching the wind blow
Joy comes in rising with the sun, with each breath I breathe
And listening to my granddaughter sing
Joy comes in so many forms
Joy can come in the form of a thunderstorm, a child's laugh,
or simply a flavored snow cone

I wish nothing but joy for you

What brings you joy?

_____

_____

_____

_____

_____

_____

_____

_____

_____

_____

_____

_____

Just a Thought...

Losing someone from your life is not always a terrible thing! Sometimes, a person can take so much from you that you lose yourself and do not even realize it. Some people just are not meant to continue with you in your life journey. Hopefully, you will recognize them and let them go!

Sometimes, losing a person is a lesson along with being a Blessing!

Robin J.

I am not open to any more bullsh@t and lies
That only leaves me teary-eyed
That only leaves me left picking up broken pieces off the
floor
That I did not even break
That only leaves heartbreak and distrust at my doorstep
And you had the audacity not even to wipe your feet

My soul needs to be nourished, so. . .
I will not sit down at the table with you any longer
Without something to eat, eat with, eat on, and a glass to
drink with . . . So that I may refresh my soul

I am worth more than your occasional text
Late-night booty calls, or no text or calls at all
Yet, you seem muddled
At my unwillingness to rush, to be in your grace
I will not undress my body
Nor my soul for any more of your half-a$$-NESS
That is only a part of your elaborate scheme, only meant to
cause delusions in my mind and sell me a pipe dream
I am not open any more to the pollution you spew that
sounds like a dream, but not one word do you mean
Leaving me hollow inside

I cannot stand by while you womanize before my eyes
While telling me you love me and tell lies after lies after lies
I am not open to allowing myself to give freely to someone
Who knows nothing of what it is to give of themselves
Only of what it is to take from me

Until I am left empty
And dangling on the edge of almost losing myself and my
mind

I am not open anymore to your misrepresentations of
yourself
And all of whom and what you say you are
Because you are too cowardly to live your true life
And refuse to own your OWN TRUTHS!
I am not open anymore to your bullsh@t and lies
That creates contempt in my eyes
And does not allow me to be who I truly am
For guarding myself against you

I am not accepting only pieces of you any longer
Because I do not give only pieces of me to you

I AM NOT OPEN TO ANY MORE BULLSH@T AND LIES...
that only leaves me teary-eyed

Robin J.

Just a Thought. . .

Don't spend too much time reflecting on what should have, could have, or would have been. Life will definitely pass you by in a blink of an eye. Don't spend too much time standing still. Keep always forward moving. Life definitely goes on with or without you!

Freedom
Is when you finally realize your worth
When you finally stop allowing people to treat you any
type of way
When you stop them from coming and going and going and
coming in your life
It is when you break the binds that bind you to someone
who is toxic
Someone whose energy drains the life out of you
Who suffocates you with their presence
Who restricts you with their emotions
Who holds you captive in the past with their baggage
When you finally get the courage
To say I have had enough
You no longer allow them
To rent space in your life for free
You start charging them for every second, every minute,
and every hour
That they attempt to steal from your life
Freedom is being free from anything or anyone
That tries to hold you down
That constrains your life or imprisons you in the past
Freedom is finally being able
To truly let go of people in your life
Who restricts you from being YOU
Who restricts your growth, your sanity
It is unshackling yourself from their world
Cutting the strings that bind you to them
It is when you get to the point where you give zero f@cks
about
What they do, say, or think
Their toxic manipulations no longer

Robin J.

Effect or affects you
You take back your power
You gain back your freedom, your life
Freedom is when you can finally let go
And it no longer disturbs your soul
Freedom is when
You no longer allow them to have control

Today, I will be free from...

_____

_____

_____

_____

_____

_____

_____

_____

_____

_____

_____

_____

_____

_____

WRITE AN ACROSTIC POEM

A poem in which the first letter of each line spells out a word, name, or phrase when read vertically.

Forward I move always
Reflecting on my life
Every moment
Every word spoken
Drowning in my emotions some days
Over thinking life at times
Moving onward trying to figure this thing called life out

Your turn. Write an acrostic poem of your own...

_____

_____

_____

_____

_____

_____

_____

_____

Robin J.

INSPIRED BY THE MOVIE "WHEN YOU SEE US"

When you see us
Tell me. . .
Why do you cross the street
Why do you clutch your purse to your side
Why does your heart skip a beat

When you see us
Tell me, what do you see . . .
What is it about us that causes you to be so mean
What makes you beat, murder, and emasculate our KINGS?

When you see us
Why does fear take control
Why is your only solution, to try and take our souls

When you see us
Why are you so hasty to dial 911
Why are you so quick to shoot with your guns
Why is it you only see a thug
Why are you constantly killing and imprisoning our sons?

When you see us
What do you see
Why do you see danger
Simply in the color of our skin

Are you an extension of your ancestors
Only in a different form
Are you the new KKK
In present
A M E R I **K K K** A
Boldly you try to destroy us
Without the white sheets
When you see us
Tell me, what do you see . . .

Robin J.

NEVER GIVE UP. . .

I hope you never ever give up on life, on love, on writing, on finding your peace, and walking in your truth, no matter how painful or hard it is at times. I hope you never ever give up on YOU!

Life is a Beautiful Blessing! Embrace it, learn from it, and throw your f@ckin' hands up, and enjoy the ride!

I will never give up on. . .

_____

_____

_____

_____

_____

_____

_____

_____

_____

_____

_____

_____

_____

_____

_____

_____

_____

_____

Robin J.

i am at times
my own worst enemy
quick to walk away from uncomfortable situations
or people
rather be alone at home, feeling sorry for myself
blaming everything on everyone else
yet not accepting blame for my part

i do, however, take responsibility
for my seclusion from the world
because i am my own worst enemy

i have become comfortable with being alone
i did not get here on my own
or from just one experience in life
all my life experiences have molded me into the woman i
am today
okay on the outside, but deep on the inside,
screamin' for someone to save me

in life, i have been taught by many people
people one would think should have known better
but because of their life experiences,
they were f@cked up and knew no better
so, they, in turn, f@cked up other people who crossed their
paths

i was taught so many negative things about myself growing
up
i was not dark enough; i was not pretty enough

i was too big-gah (not knowing back then that thick would
be in)
i was made to feel less than, so i always wanted more
more color, coarser hair, more friends, more love
because i am my own worst enemy

often, i reflect on how i got to this place
lonely on the inside
trying to bandage the scars with smiles
so i can hide the anger, the pain, the bitterness
i feel on the inside
and cannot seem to let go of
blaming everyone but myself
for this self-hate that i feel for myself

i am my own worst enemy
for not allowing myself to live in my truths
for not addressing it sooner
for putting band-aids on all my open wounds
i constantly crumbled it up
and placed it safely deep within the pits of my soul
only to pull it out when i am alone
and do absolutely nothing with it

i am my own worst enemy
allowing what others thought of me
to mold me into something and someone i am not
only ever wanting to be totally free
and be who God intended me to be

Robin J.

i am my own worst enemy
i am so good at putting on a show
i smile, and in those moments, i forget about the pain
until i am left alone again
with nothing but my thoughts
from the past

all that i have given
all the betrayal from so-called family and friends
i often question
has my living been in vain
is there no end to this self-inflected pain
i am my own worst enemy

giving up on myself before i even got started
not even giving life, love, or friendships a chance
because i have become so guarded
i am my own worst
e n e m y

Kiss me with kisses that taste like truth
Look at me with eyes of fire and like I am the only woman
you desire
Hold me tight with arms that would never let me fall
Speak to me with words to help mend my damaged soul
Promise to be there
Could you do that
Would you do that
Could you truly love me and kiss me with truths

Robin J.

If we wrote everything we thought down for the world to
see, I imagine the world would be covered in words of . . .

Pain and Pleasure,
Distrust and Loyalty

Relationships and Situationships
Marriage and Divorce
Faith and Unbelieving
Laughter and Tears
Family and Fam-enemies,
Friends and Frien-enemies
Justice and Injustice
Lies and Honesty
Love and Hate
Life and Death
Peace and Conflict
Selfishness and Selflessness,
Blackism and Racism

Words filled with all the emotions we have all experienced
From all the bullsh@t and good sh@t we have encountered
along our journey called LIFE.

It would be covered in a canvas of words
Touching every emotion we have ever felt
And maybe some we have yet to experience
Words that may touch someone's soul (I pray they do)
Words that may offend others, helpful to some

And there will be those who it just won't resonate with
At the end of the day, though
They would be your words expressing your thoughts and
your emotions
Written on your canvas
Every word, every line, written down
Inked with your love, passion, encouragement, and
sometimes pain and anger, but all written by you and me
for the world to see!

Robin J.

You can get stuck in Life!
Stuck with the same old attitude
Stuck with the same old job
Stuck with the same old daily routine
Stuck with the same old perceptions of life
Stuck with the same old hurts from the past
Stuck with the same old pains you keep holding on to
Stuck with the same old addictions that destroy you
Stuck with the same old negativity that hinders you
Stuck with the same old blame game of its everybody else
fault but yours
Stuck with the same old feeling of being not good enough
Stuck with the same old feeling of failing, so you don't try
Stuck with the same old feeling of rejection
Stuck with the same old feeling of needing to be accepted
Stuck with the same old feeling of wanting someone to save
you, but you are not even willing to save yourself
Stuck with the same old attitude that you're always right

Stuck with the same old feeling of not loving the most
important person in this world…YOURSELF!

Just stuck in the past, and it keeps you hostage there
Just stuck in the same ole same ole

Being stuck is holding you back.
When are you going to get unstuck and live your life?

Today, I found a peace I have never known
As the boat bounces on top of the choppy waves
A feeling of calm flows through my body and mind
The wind blowing as sprinkles of water splash my face
Reminding me that I am alive and all will be well

That I am free
That I choose what affects me
Today was a good day

Write about a moment of peace and how it made you feel...

_____

_____

_____

_____

_____

_____

_____

_____

_____

Robin J.

I was something you were not prepared for
I told you
I am not your average storm
Even sent out a weather advisory
Hours, days, weeks before
You said you could deal with the little wind and rain
That would be coming your way
You did not take cover
Did not board up your heart
Did not prepare for days with no lights
You came with just an umbrella
Little did you know
My wind gusts, storm surges, thunder, and lightning
Would be too much for that frail umbrella you came
equipped with
Thinking it could weather my storms
And all that was even before my actual hurricane came
ashore!

Robin J.

I am f@cked up
I know
But I can't control it
I don't know
That I even want to
It is easier being
This way
I should probably have a
▲ caution sign
Or something flashing
((((Yellow))))
On my forehead
Warning anyone that comes near to beware
And enter at your own risk
Life would be so much more simplified
If we all just came with
Warning Signs

I am a product of my self-doubt

This foolish mind of mine keeps me trapped
Keeps me making misconceptions about life
That causes me turmoil

Me

Choosing to stay
Lost in a cesspool of emotions

Me

Choosing to stay off-track
Tattered from lost loves
That were never meant to be

Me

Choosing to stay
Dispirited by broken promises
Never kept
Of Loves that would never last
Broken is my heart like shard glass
Shattered by my thoughts that
Someone, anyone would care enough to actually love me
Would care enough to help me mend all my broken pieces
and save me from myself

Robin J.

Me

Foolish to think someone would
Foolish to think someone could
Foolish mind of mine

You crept up on me like a thief in the night
You blurred my vision of this battle I was to fight
Took all of my strength and gave me no hope
Left me in fear of what was to come
Would I be around for a long life with my sons

Didn't feel this was right
So many days, I did not want to go on
Wanted so badly to give up the fight
And slip quietly into the night

You, YOU
Left me broken, left me bruised
Left me scared and confused
Left me dazed and wondering what I was going to do
Thought this was it
That this was the BIG one the second time around
I knew I had so much more to give life

One day, I heard someone say
Get your a$$ up and fight
No more crying, no more lying in bed
No more feeling sorry for yourself
Get up and get dressed
And show it you're one step ahead
You crept up on me
Did not see you coming
Was terrified of this fight
Thought I was done, thought you had won
Until I realized I had so much more life to live
So, I crept up on you

Robin J.

Like a theft in the night
I took back my life
And won this fight
#CancerSucks

Truth is, I am not perfect, nor will I ever be
Truth is, I sometimes get in my own way, and I am learning
that it is okay
Truth is, my mouth is slick, and at times, I do not know all
the right things to say
Truth is, I hold my tongue about a lot of things I want to
express; I have learned it's best
Truth is, I sometimes get angry when things do not go my
way
Truth is, I find it easy just to walk away
Truth is, sometimes, when I am alone, I cry because I get
overwhelmed with life
Truth is, the past sometimes still hurts deep down inside
Truth is, I have started learning to put me first
Truth is, I have never been a size 8, and I have learned that
that is okay
Truth is, I think I am sexy anyway
Truth is, some days my hair is a mess, and I may not dress
my best
Truth is, some days I could care less
Truth is, I never really believed in love
Truth is, I am scared to love and be loved
Truth is, my baggage some days is my best friend
Truth is, I have a tough time letting people in
Truth is, I do not have many friends
Truth is, I am cool with not fitting in
Truth is, I am such a homebody
Truth is, Because I don't trust anybody
Truth is, I do sometimes need somebody
Truth is, I am terrified to begin again

Robin J.

Truth is, I do not know where my journey will end
Truth is, I am just like you, and you are just like me
Truth is, some days I have questioned God
Truth is, I know because of him, I am still here
Truth is, these are some of my Truths, and they have set me free
Truth is, do you know what your truth is?

My Truth Is...

_____

_____

_____

_____

_____

_____

_____

_____

_____

_____

_____

_____

Always remember to tell those you care about how much they mean to you. Remember, it is not always about the grand things someone does for you or that you do for someone. Sometimes, it's about all the little considerate things we do for one another that show how much we care—things we tend to take for granted!

I just wanted to say I love you
And I am sorry if I make you feel any other way
I appreciate all that you do
That's why my love runs so deep for you
I sometimes forget to show you
I sometimes forget to say
Things I know I should
Like, thank you for giving the boys a bath
Like, thank you for taking out the trash
Thank you for keeping all the bills paid
And putting up with me on my worst days
Maybe my kisses and words are not enough
To reassure you of my love
But there is no other place I would rather be
Then here with you and our family
Without you in my life, it just would not be complete
So, at those times, I do not say what I should
Or maybe the expression on my face you misunderstood
I hope that within your heart
You know that you are a very important part
That makes our life complete
And without you, there would be no me
And that I will love you throughout eternity

Robin J.

This feeling is awe-inspiring
The way you love me
During the rain
The way you protect me
In my pain
The way you reassure me
That all will be okay
The way you make me feel beautiful
Even on my bad days
How you never let me down
Even when I put your love to the test
The way you always listen
Even when I am being a pest
For you to love me through all my flaws and at my best
Through all my insecurities and mess
For you to catch me when I am spiraling down
You're there for me
Every single time I fall
And for me, that says it all

I imagine making love with words would be like. . .
Floating in the air amid the beautiful clouds
With small **adjectives** falling onto our bodies
Penetrating our skin with every **vowel**
A E I O U and sometimes Y
As we partake in the breathtaking view of the sunrise
With all its rays of morning glory
Shining each **syllable** bright into our eyes
I imagine long, winding mountain roads that never end
That wrap around our souls with every **sentence** spoken
Or maybe a soft blanket of snow gently covering our bodies
with every **phrase**
Each **verb** prickling every inch of our skin with never-
ending rapture
I imagine making love with words would be like magic
with you
The sweet taste of that just ripe cherry
All the **nouns** trickling from the corners of our lips
You tasting mine, me tasting yours
I imagine making love with words would be like **adverbs**
gripping the sheets, **pronouns** making our legs weak, and
conjunctions pouring down our bodies as our words
entwine, making love with our intelligent minds.

Robin J.

Her curves and rough edges
The fullness of her hips
The way she always has a plan
And makes do with what she can
Her elegance and grace
No matter what the world throws her way,
She always handles it with a smile on her face
That's a Woman of Grace!

You can find beauty in such small things
Like lightning flashing across the clouds
Its beauty in the sparks of light glimmering
Through the clouds and night skies

Robin J.

One day, I will be just a faded memory
Of someone you once knew
Someone who once loved you for you
One day, you will reflect back and remember my scent
You will remember what I tasted like on your lips
You will remember the way my body felt on yours
      and how my silly little quirky ways made you smile
You will remember all I ever wanted was the best for you
And one day, you will reach for me,
      but I won't be there
Because when you had me,
      you didn't bother to show you cared

Can you feel me
I am close to your soul, can you feel me now
Can you reach out and touch the soft skin on my face
Run your fingers through the curls of my hair
Can you feel your hands around my waist
They fit so perfectly there, pulling me near
Can you feel my breath as I softly kiss your neck
Can you hear my whispers as you drift off to sleep
When you close your eyes, do you see me
Do you envision your hand in mine, our bodies entwined

Can you feel my love sliding down on you
I know you do; I am so versed in everything about you
I am so in tune with your being, with your soul
I know what you are pondering
I can feel your heartbeat from miles away
I anticipate each word you say

I am a part of you, nothing you can do to erase me
You fight it at every turn; you want me to leave, to forget
my essence
But down deep in the abyss of your soul, you long for my
presence
Your eyes say all the things you dare not; that is why you
turn away

You keep me at a distance, protecting yourself
From jumping off the edge to a place there is no coming
back from

Robin J.

You want me close
But you dare not give in to the seduction of my words, my
voice, or my world
You safeguard your thoughts and words
For fear of my infiltration into your world, into your heart.
But I am there whether you want me or not
There is no letting me go; I am embedded in your soul
Can you feel me?

WORD PROMPT!

Thewless *– lacking morals or virtue. Lacking vigor or energy; listless; weak; nerveless.*

He was a **thewless** person, not caring how he mistreated anyone— seeming to be numb to the pain he caused. Acting as if he was above it all.

Use the word *thewless* in a poem of your own...

_____

_____

_____

_____

_____

_____

_____

_____

_____

_____

Robin J.

He is a sweet addiction
Always leaves me
Fienin' for more
He makes me feel
Everything I knew I was
He believes in me
When no one else does
He gives me the desire to
Be again
To love again

His words
His touch
The way he allows me to
Uniquely just be me
No judgment
No expectations
No conditions
No restrictions
Yes! He is my sweetest addiction
I feel him running through my veins
One hit and I was done

Strung out
On his love

Your love
Is like the ocean waves
Sweeping in like a roar
Then, in one breath
Sweeping back out from shore!

Robin J.

I wonder what love feels like?
Does it feel like
Floating in the ocean
While looking up at the stars

Does it feel like
Sitting on a bench in the park,
Eyes closed, feeling the wind
Blow across your face

Or maybe it feels like your very
First kiss

Does it feel like those things they call butterflies
In the pit of your stomach
Fluttering up
Like hot lava from a volcano

I wonder does it feel like this
Does it feel like that soft kiss on your neck
That makes your body quiver

Or is it the feeling of your heart beating out your chest
Whenever they come near you.

That feeling of their hand softly touching your body
Exploring every flawed inch

Or does it feel like being serenaded with the words you spit
in your poetry verse
Keeping me captured in your essence, hanging off every
syllable

Is love that deep look into each other's eyes?
No words spoken, but all is understood
I am sure love feels like all of these things and more

Robin J.

In the morning dew
I rush to you
Gentle breeze across my face
Sun prickling my skin
Anticipating your embrace

WORD PROMPT!

Beware *– to be on guard against; be cautious of*

All the warning signs were there
I entered willingly, hoping I could change him
Make him whole again
Little did I know he would take my soul
And leave me entangled in bitterness, anger, and discontent
Everything told me to **beware**
All the warning signs were there
But I entered willingly, and now we are here

Your turn! Use the word *beware* in a poem...

_____

_____

_____

_____

_____

_____

_____

_____

_____

Robin J.

My love for you is like this battle between my heart and mind.
Pulling me into complex pieces, pieces you know all too well.

Sometimes feeling like I should just leave it all behind.
Throw up my hands and chuck you the peace sign, but with you is where I want to be.

Needing you like it is essential to my being, like every breath I breathe.

Loving you more than life itself.

Your love, though, is always constantly putting me to the test. Should I stay, or should I leave.

I fell in love with you because you love the worst of me and allowed me to love the worst of you.

Without conditions or restrictions or limitations to our love.

Together, we are our best definition of love.

Our love is so rare. It is that love kryptonite that leaves you on your knees.

With a needle in your veins, I would take it, even if you were a dare.

When my hair is a mess,
Would you still love me?

When I'm having one of my many bad days,
Could you still love me?

When I can't seem to get it together,
Would you still love me

If I gain a little weight,
Could you still love me

If I was broke and homeless,
Would you still love me

When my outer beauty starts to fade,
Could you still love me

If I broke your heart,
Would you still love me

If I am fussing 'cause the bills are past due,
Would you still love me

If I stop making sweet love to you,
Would you still love me

If ever I get sick and can't take care of myself,
Could you still love me

Robin J.

Can you love me
When I am not at my best
Would you still love me?
Could you still love me?

When everything about me puts you to the test,
Would you still love me?

Even when I am not at my best

It will take your heart
Then it will tear . . . it apart
Into pieces

Trust thrown right out the door
Tears spill onto your pillow
Leaves you feeling empty
It steals your soul
Devours your life
It keeps you up late at night
Hanging on for dear life

Deceiving
It arouses your love
Makes you feel secure
Then
. . . it cuts like a knife

But it feels so good
When it is right

Robin J.

Can we just sit and talk?
Wait, let me get a pen and some paper
Just want to take some notes
So I can get to know you
With each pen stroke
I want to save them for later
So I can read back all your hopes and dreams
And memorize all of what makes you a King

His Poetic Kisses
She longed for
Soft lips with
Poetic intelligence free flowing from them

His kisses were
Something she had dreamed of all her life
Soft and Sensual
His Poetic Kisses are

The way he brushed her hair away
From the soft frame of her face

The warmth of his breath on her neck
Caused flutters in her stomach
As he pulled her near

The taste of him
Was more than her wildest dreams could have ever
imagined

Her whole body tingled
From the touch of his hands on the small of her back

His presence calmed her spirit
It was as if time had stopped
No one else existed
But she and him

Visions of growing old with someone were there
Where they had not been before
A lifetime of Poetic Kisses is what she wanted

Robin J.

The very moment his lips met hers
His tongue traced her lips
She quivered
He was generous
He was passionate and intentional with
Each poetic kiss
Tactfully made to form beautiful, complex emotions

She found somebody who
Awakened her soul
She was besotted with one kiss
To his Poetic Kisses

Do you feel the aura of my words
The way they spill out of my soft lips onto his hench frame
My lips ingrained in his memory forever
A diary only he can read
Addicted to my words

I love the way

His eyes scan my body like a canvas
That is an essential piece of his being

In his eyes, I see the desire
He needs me
Like I need him

My words flow into him like a love letter
Being written with every word piercing his soul

His fingertips scan every inch of me
His touch is like a frigid wind gushing through
unexpectedly
It shivers me to my core

His words speak life
My words speak yearning

He has an appetite for my words
That I eagerly feed him
And we
...end the night with a poem he helped create

Robin J.

WRITE AN ACROSTIC POEM

A poem in which the first letter of each line spells out a word, name, or phrase when read vertically.

She was beautiful inside and out
Walked with confidence
Addressed situations with elegance
Noticed by all when she entered a room
Knowing her worth she eluded style and distinction

Your turn. Write an acrostic poem of your own...

_____

_____

_____

_____

_____

_____

_____

_____

I want to touch your SOUL
Make you feel like a KING
Because . . . YOU'RE so worth it

Love on all your rough edges
Reassure you
I am here forever
Loving you through it all
Whatever life may bring your way
Inspire you to be a better man
Take time to listen when you're talkin'
Help you with your dreams and plans
Reassure you I understand
Because . . . YOU'RE so worth it

I see what is hidden behind your eyes
Things you do not want the world to see
Things you try to hide
Just know you can trust me with your demons
Allow me to help you heal your soul
Always will be there when you need me most
Because . . . YOU'RE so worth it

I will never switch up
Will always love you, even at your worst
Perfect I am not, though perfect I am for you
And perfect you are for me
Let me remind you daily that YOU ARE A KING
Be your peace and your Queen
Let me touch your soul
Make you feel like a KING
Because . . . YOU'RE so Worth it!

Robin J.

Happy Anniversary

I am so glad we have made it this far
You were a divine inspiration when my life was falling apart
You saved me from myself when I had no one else
You gave me love when I could not even love myself

Life has thrown us some curveballs
But we have stood tall, stride for stride
We have weathered many storms
In our darkest hours, you stood tall and strong
Encouraged me to keep pressing on

This life has not been easy for us, you never skipped a beat
Knowing all the right things to say and do
Showing me mad, crazy love, never budging, even when I
screamed, "F@ck you! I'm through!"
You've been that one constant and steady thing in my life
Our love has flourished during this crazy thing we call life
I am so glad you made me your wife
You are my shining star, when everything around us is dark
You are my pick-me-up when I am feeling unsure of life
My rock, my king, my everything
You give me mad love, always slow and steady
I appreciate you for loving me, for providing for me
for protecting me, for understanding me
for listening to me, for encouraging me
for leading me, for supporting me
for being my BEST FRIEND
for showing me what unconditional love is
And I am so glad to be called your wife
Happy Anniversary, Baby

She is everything she was not without him
He makes her complete
He compliments her
In ways that give her a radiant glow
For all the world to see
Never disrespectful
Never has her guessing
Where she stands in his life
He keeps her happy
With thoughtful gestures of love
He loves the smile in her eyes
He does everything he can to keep it there
He is all she ever wanted in a man, desired in a friend, and
longed for in a lover
She is everything she was not without him
It excites her
The way he gazes upon her full frame
It gives her life
Makes her feel
His eyes are only for her
Makes her feel like the most beautiful woman in the world
In his world
The way his hands perfectly etch her body
Like he has known her all her life
While speaking life into her essence
He reassures her that everything will fall into place
When she has doubts about life
He is there with all the right words to say
He stands by her side, stride for stride
Allowing her space

Robin J.

Allowing her to feel safe
Allowing her to unveil her demons
Without worry of him using them against her
Exploring her wildest dreams
But still
Protecting her with his last breath
Allowing her to constantly be her at best

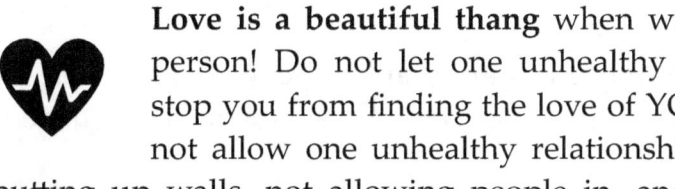 **Love is a beautiful thang** when with the right person! Do not let one unhealthy relationship stop you from finding the love of YOUR life. Do not allow one unhealthy relationship have you putting up walls, not allowing people in, and constantly reinforcing it so you don't get hurt again. We do not just find love because of where we may be looking or not looking for it. And it damn sure is hard to find love when trying to see over walls we have built up. Walls not only do not allow people in, but they do not allow you out! Love is hard because we make it hard. But love is beautiful when with the right person.

Robin J.

L O V E

What does love look like?

It looks like a morning sunrise after a heavy rain, shining
through the beautiful storm clouds as they move unhurried
across the sky

What does love sound like?

It sounds like a soulful, smooth harmony that awakens the
best parts of you, has you snapping your fingers to the
rhythmic beats of life

What does love feel like?

It feels like peace in a room full of confusion.

What does love LOOK like to me?

_____

_____

_____

_____

What does love SOUND like to me?

_____

_____

_____

_____

What does love FEEL like to me?

_____

_____

_____

_____

Robin J.

I want that part of you
That you refuse to give to anyone
That you hide from the world
Because you are not certain how it will react to you
Just being 100% you
That part of you that you only share with yourself
That part of you that only comes out when you are alone
When you think no one is looking
That part of you that had a difficult day
And feels like giving up
That part of you that knows the bills are coming due
And you're stressed out on figuring out what to do
That you that is still hurt from childhood pain
That you that cries in the middle of the night
Because life just is not going right
That you that still carries around baggage
Because you haven't learned to set it down and let it go
I want that you
That talks all night about your dreams and fears
That is not afraid to shed tears
That you that you even doubt sometimes
That you that always manages to shine
I want that you, that you do not give to anyone else
I want the best of you and nothing else

I would love to find
The love of my life
I would not fight it
There would be no running from it
I would let the feelings flow freely
Open arms to embrace it
Sweet lips to taste it
A love that is good for my soul

Robin J.

I'm complicated
BUT
You love me anyway
When my hair is a mess
You gently brush it away
On my silent days
You know just what to say

Sometimes, I'm mouthy
And I get on your nerves
I pout on my bad days
There are times I don't know
How to fully express myself

My thoughts get jumbled
Can't always find the words to say
But you
You love me anyway

Complexity is my normal
From day to day
Constantly
I get in my own way
You, though,   You always

ALWAYS. . .let me know it's ok
You love me anyway

I Love that 80's/90's . . .YOU!
That Members Only
My Adidas . . .YOU
Rockin' the latest Con's
With your Kangol hat and Phat gold chains. . .YOU!
That Smooth Operator
'Cause you always Make 'Em Say Ugh. . .YOU!
I love that
How you like me now
'Cause you have all the girls Hypnotized
When you stare them in their eyes
Lick your lips and give them that crooked smile
That Rock the Bells cause It's Tricky
Your love is so deep. . .YOU!
'Cause It Takes Two
That you that needs an Around the Way Girl
With Bamboo earrings at least two pairs
That how you make me feel
I Need Love, cause I'm the one for you
That Bump n' Grind
And I Don't See Nothing Wrong. . .YOU!
That Yo that sh@t is whack
That YOU, you know what you do
That make it do what it do
Yeah! I love that 80's/90's . . .You
The way you Express Yourself
That Fight the Power . . .YOU!
'Cause It Takes Two to make things go right
That Supersonic, Cause you're the King of Rock
There is none higher . . .YOU!

Robin J.

Got me singing Whatta Man, Whatta Man
What a Mighty Man
That I'm so in love, with all the things you do!
I love that 80's/90's . . .YOU!

Booty
Round, Voluptuous
Thick, Phat
Stretch marks
Yep, like 'em like that

Dimples
Apple bottom, Derriere, Caboose
Make it wiggle
Bounce it up and down
Smack it and watch it jiggle

Bootylicious…oh my!
There's power in that round mound
Has some men out here becoming Bootyologist
And bowing down

Make it clap to the beat
Watch those knees get weak
Mesmerized by the way they work it; I mean, twerk it
It is perfect if it has
That just right jiggle to it

Junk in the trunk
Make a man search through it
Damn, girl, the way it looks in those jeans
Curvaceous and tempting from seam to seam
The way it sways from left to right

Natural is the best way
But ain't complaining either way
Wanna put your hands on it

Robin J.

Grab it, Smack it, Rub it down
Maybe even lay your head on it
Catch some Z's for a while
Not all are equal
It comes in all different shapes and sizes
Full-Figured, Mid-Size, or Small
As long as it is round
Men love them all
Left Cheek, Right Cheek or Both Cheeks
That booty makes men weak

Healing — *"the process of making or becoming sound or healthy again"*

Healing is a process, and it does not happen overnight. When you get to a place where that person, situation, or circumstance no longer effects or affects you and you no longer allow it your energy, you are on the road to healing.

Healing for me is...

_____

_____

_____

_____

_____

_____

_____

_____

_____

_____

_____

Robin J.

Memories of you come flooding back into my mind
There is a part of me that will never forget you
As much as I might want to and try to
Seems my mind will always hold on to
The part of you that I first met
The part of you I don't regret
Oh, how those memories will not let me forget
That I longed for something you could never give
Now, I am left trying to mend the broken pieces
And keep it all together
I don't think I saw there was no forever
And how you were no good for me
Maybe I did, but just didn't want to see
How could I forget all the times you made me laugh
The times you made me weep and left me broken
No, I don't think I could ever forget you
As much as I try to, as much as I long to
Those memories, at times, come flooding back into my
mind
At times, I still feel you
Your hands tracing down the small of my back
Your lips softly kissing the side of my neck
I still see your smile and catch a whiff of your cologne
I recall all the small, considerate things you did
How could I forget you?
Etched in my mind, you will always be a part of me
unfortunately
I try but can't forget all the good times
Seems they outweigh all the bad

Even when you made me miserable, and I could not stand
you
Something gravitated me back towards you
Pulling me back like a bad habit
Back to the days I adored you and would go to hell and
back for you
I do not think my heart will ever let me forget you
I cannot ignore, though, the times you laid me to the side as
if I were a waste of time
To satisfy your guilty pleasures of never-ending lies after
lies
Yes, memories of you come flooding back into my mind
My head can't ignore the times you hurt my pride
You made a fool of me, and I could never understand why
Though my heart will not let me forget, my mind stops me
from succumbing to your charm
No, I don't think my heart will ever let me forget you
As much as I want to
As much as I need to
My mind stops me from falling again for you
It stops me from returning to that you that is not good for
me
Memories of you come flooding back into my mind

Robin J.

The **SECOND** I stretched out my arms to you
Was the second you decided to be untrue
The **MINUTE** I opened up to you
Was the minute it became no trust, no love
The **HOUR** I gave my heart to you
Was the hour you decided to be untrue
The **DAY** I confessed my love for you
Was the day you said you loved me, too
The **WEEK** I couldn't do for you
Was the week you said I was never good enough for you
The **MONTH** I needed you to hold me down
Was the month you checked out but still stayed around
The **YEAR** I cried and thought I would die
Was the year you finally said goodbye

It was never meant to be
You and me
There was no trust
From the very beginning
Just a whole lot of what we thought was love
Passion that could not be measured
But what is love or passion with
No trust
Just
L u s t

Robin J.

DISTANCE

"Dedicated to Pita"

He was always my biggest weakness
Even from a distance
I dreamed of a house on the hill
Below the stars
Filled with happiness, love, and our scars
But that was something he and me
Perceived differently
He was young, wild, and free
I was unsure but steady on my feet
Chaos was a very good friend to us
We were just not meant to be
I held on as long as I could
I took what pieces of him I could
Things just eventually got misunderstood
Distance slipped between us
In the blanket of night
He was gone from my sight
And all I could do was only love him from a distance
If time were on our side
I'm sure we would have gone stride for stride
I am positive things would have turned out different
Although now I can only continue loving him from a distance

APOLOGY!

I think I have tried a thousand times
To apologize, to say I am sorry
In my mind I have rehearsed it over and over again
I just seem not to get it right
Time has slipped by—weeks, months, and years
Our lives have moved past that time
I don't even think you think of me anymore
In my mind, I have said I am sorry like a broken record
A thousand times over and over and over
Always drifting back to that moment
When I should have said, could have said, "I'm sorry"
I should have called
I should have looked for you
I should have said or done something . . . Anything
Playing it over and over in my head like a broken record
The words of all my apologies to you
For the lies I told to you, for all the things I did and didn't
do
For my actions that caused you to drift away
I have apologized to you a thousand times
In my mind, I never got it right
I do not know if you would care to hear my words now
I do not know if they would even soak through to you
I cannot imagine how you feel
So much time has passed
Even though I never uttered the words
Now I would not even know where to start
I only know my apology would come from the heart

Robin J.

BAD DAYS!

I am sure we all have BAD days, some of us more than others. Learn that it is OK to have BAD days. You are human.

Just do not let those BAD days have YOU!

Somedays, I let my emotions get the best of me
Not knowing the appropriate way to handle them
I sometimes lose sight of my emotional responsibilities
Of staying in my own lane
Somedays, I really don't give a f@ck
About being responsible emotionally

Robin J.

I never understood your mistreatment of me
Why you couldn't just let us go
Why you couldn't just love me
I never understood your built-up anger
The disgust in your eyes
Seems it was only directed towards me
How could you be so diabolical
So unsympathetic
To someone who only wanted to love you
To someone who held you down
When it was only us
And no one else around

But I am still here

I was there when you had absolutely nothing or no one
When you were just a shell of yourself
Trying to find yourself in this cold world
Falling over your own two left feet
But I couldn't compete
With what was going on inside you

But I am still here

You ripped open wounds so deep
And poured salt on them
While you watched me weep
You beat me down with your words
Made me feel as if I had no value
And there was no healing for me

But I am still here

106

And I absolutely would have given my life for you
I saw in you what you did not see in yourself
But you
See, you never saw my worth
You were only in it for your own self-worth
For your own gain and my pain
I will never understand your mistreatment of me

But I am still here

I am baffled by why you stayed around so long
Why you wasted years of my life
Your intentions were never genuine
Your love was never trustworthy
Your motives were always suspect

But I am still here

You were never fully devoted or committed to us, to me
You were present, but you were not mentally there
You checked out long ago
And it does not seem fair
You did everything to break me
Make me feel unworthy
Yet, after all the tears and years,
I am still here

I can't afford to absorb any more of your bullsh@t
Any more of your "Baby I'm sorry" and "I didn't mean to
do it"
I've got to start putting myself first

Robin J.

Take the scissors and cut all ties
And learn to better love myself more
Starting with Self-Love, Self-Care, and being Selfish as
F@ck!

What self-care practices can you start doing to nourish your mind, body and soul? Examples: meditation, exercise, walks and self-compassion.

_____

_____

_____

_____

_____

_____

_____

_____

_____

_____

_____

_____

Distant thoughts of you hang around my heart,
With my mind being weakened,
Taunted by the absence of your presence
Confused by the steady intrusion of you
Consumed with my delusion of what we could have been
Trapped by my love for you
When will these thoughts ever end

Robin J.

I feel you in my sleep
I wake up to find you not here
I lay there
Hands on my stomach
Sweating
Wondering
Was I dreaming
Were you really here
Everything felt so real
Your kiss
Your caress
I feel you all the time
In my mind
In my dreams
Throughout my days
The unmistakable smell of you
Reality is
You're only a thought. . .a daydream
But I feel you
I swear, I see you at a glance
I sit smiling across the table at you
I cuddle up at night with you
Your presence is all around me
Reminding me constantly of what I miss
Like clouds in the sky
That drift quickly by
You're there; I see you
Though I could never reach you
Never physically able to touch you
We always in the end

Get what we deserve
I deserve to have these never-ending thoughts of you
Waking up
Not next to you

Robin J.

Alone with my thoughts of you
Of all that we will never be
I see happy couples, smiling couples
And wonder if they are genuinely happy
Or is that just a façade like we used to be

With you, I was happy in the beginning
The happiness slowly turned to misery, followed by despair
I wonder if I had known in the beginning
You were not who and what you portrayed yourself to be
Would I have stayed
I imagine I would have

You had a way that was so
Charming,
Intoxicating,
So very captivating

I wonder if thoughts of me, of us
Ran through your mind
In that moment, when we completely lost it all

It seems like yesterday
You and I were happy in fake love

Nothing I did was good enough
Nothing I ever said was right
But you swore you loved me
Forever is what you said

I don't weep anymore,
There is nothing to weep for

Everything I ever wanted disappeared slowly
Like the sun setting and pouring darkness onto my life

I miss you at times
I won't even lie to myself; I do
I think of all the times you made me feel worthless
I think of all the nights, waiting up for you
Only to fall asleep and to wake up to find you still not there
I never thought you could be present in a relationship but
not be present But you showed me it was possible

I fell for you hard
Now I sit here with scars

I thought I knew what love was
Until I got that first black eye
The push down the stairs
I felt like you really cared
The chokehold
The kicks
The bloody lips
I took every lick
Thinking it was love

I sit alone with my thoughts now
I don't even remember the shots
I wish I could take it all back
But we are both alone now in the dark

Robin J.

When you love someone
How could you...
        Cheat on them
   Lie to them
         Hurt them
         Neglect them
       Abuse them
Verbally, mentally, or physically assault them
Look into their eyes, SMILE, and tell them "I love you"

In my haste, I forgot who you really were
I let you back in
Knowing deep in my heart
You would never change
That each time I allowed you back
I would be hurting myself all over again
One cannot blame you
Because I already knew all the dangers of you

Robin J.

He learned all my secrets
My scars
My fears
My flaws
My complexities
My tragedies
And then he used them
Against me!

You and I
I know
We are no good
For each other
As much as I hate to admit

You, with your trust issues
Me, with my insecurities
And then everything else
That's caught in the middle

It wouldn't work

No matter how much
I believe we are soul ties
Maybe just maybe
We could find a way

I know, though,
We are no good for each other
It doesn't stop me from
Thinking of the what-ifs
The could haves
And should haves
It doesn't stop my
Daydreams of us

Sometimes, I lay in bed
And I swear I feel you
Cuddled up
Next to me
Your arms wrapped

Robin J.

Around me
You whispering
In my ear
"I love you"
Me feeling safe in your arms

Sometimes, I sit at work
And daydream about
Days spent with you
Talking for hours
Nights spent
Making love to you
Loving everything about us

I love seeing you smile
We're happy in my daydreams

Some soul ties are not meant to be
Like you and me
Some are meant
To be for that moment in life
Though you'll always be connected
You sometimes have to LET GO
Break the ties that bind you

Because it's not meant for us to be
You and I

I admit
You almost had me
I admit
I was almost there
I was swimming
In your words
Almost drowned
Until I came up for air

Here we go again
Same old song again
Playing on the radio

I admit
I miss you
I admit
I will always care
I admit I'm a fool for you
Just wondering if you ever really cared

I admit I'm movin' on
I admit you're no good for me
I admit

You + Me = Emotional Anguish
And it could never be

Robin J.

WORD PROMPT!

Arcane — known or understood by very few; mysterious; secret.

He didn't speak much
His eyes said way more than he ever could
He moved in silence
But so much was just understood
Such an **arcane** type of man he is
Leaves you wanting to explore more of his world

Your turn! Use the word *arcane* in a poem...

For a minute, you had me
Hangin' on your every word
Lost for a while
In your presence
In your essence
I slipped
Forgot for a second
Who you used to be
And
Who you really are
Is who you will always be to me
Everything about you
Spoke change
I fell for the distraction
Then I realized
For you, it was just a game
A get-back
From past mistakes
For a minute, you had me
Just like you did
Back then
Though, this time, I win

Robin J.

WRITE A HAIKU POEM USING THE WORD "BEAUTIFUL"

A haiku poem is composed of only 3 lines. The first line of the haiku has 5 syllables, the second line has 7 syllables, and the third has 5 syllables.

Beautiful things come
And beautiful things will go
Just be beautiful

Your turn. Write a haiku poem of your own...

_____

_____

_____

_____

_____

_____

_____

It starts with seconds
Then turns to minutes
Which turns to hours
That eventually turn into days
Then weeks
Followed by months
And then years go by
That we don't speak
That we don't hear
That we don't see
That we don't touch
That we don't feel
That we don't try to understand

And then we wonder
Why
It fell apart

Robin J.

He came in like a beautiful tornado

He was beautiful to gaze upon from a distance

All menacing and dark, he was mysterious

He was charming; he left her weak

He left nothing but destruction

And HEARTBREAK

At her doorstep

He was not

The average man

You would meet

On any street

He left

Nothing but

A path of

Destruction

And a whirlwind of confusion everywhere he went

I notice you from the corner of the room
You not knowing I was there
But, for a second, I thought you caught my stares

I watched you as you moved around the room
Taking in small conversations
Laughing at unfunny jokes
Licking your lips and flashing that signature smile
I remember those lips so well, how they felt

I see you still have
That charismatic charm that draws people in

I noticed every once in a while
You looked down at your watch
And then towards the door
Wonder who you're waiting for

I could hear your laughs from across the room
I remember that laugh like it was yesterday

In all your small talk, not once did you notice I was there
Not once did you notice my stares
So wrapped up in being the life of the party

I remember you so well I remember your essence
The way you walked, the way you talked
The way you made everything okay
Seems like it was so long ago

I loved your smile
Gosh, I hadn't seen it in a long while

Robin J.

So badly I want to walk up and say,
"Hi! How have you been?"
But do I dare
I do not think any words would flow out of my mouth

I see you glancing at your watch and the door again
I wonder what her name is,
I know it's a her
Wonder . . .
What she looks like
Does she do it better than me
Is she prettier than me

Guess that is none of my business

I didn't notice her at first
Until you grabbed her by the waist
Gave her that same embrace you used to give me
Chills ran through me, jealousy consumed me
I shouldn't have given up, shouldn't have walked away
Can't imagine how things would have turned out
If I had stayed
Toxic . . .
You and me
It was never meant to be

Just a Thought. . .

Sometimes we give so much of ourselves that we forget about the most important person. . .Self

Don't be afraid to be unapologetic about doing what's best for you and taking care of YOURSELF!

Taking care of yourself is not selfish. It's necessary for your well-being. . . Self-Care. . . Self-Love. . . Selfish.

Robin J.

I fell for him
No pad to brace my fall
No parachute
That would drift me down
Safely
To the ground

I sabotaged our ending this time
Making sure I did and said all the things that would
Turn YOU off, Piss YOU off
Make YOU want to call it quits this time

This time, it would not be me
Who rejected you, it would be you rejecting me
It would not be me causing you any pain, disappointment,
and feelings of rejection
It would not be you saying
"This isn't working" or "I don't want this anymore"

This needed to end
But this time it would be on your terms
And you who rejected me
I could not bear to cause you any more pain

If I made you end it with me
It would set me at ease
That I did not cause you any heartbreak
Any more layers of disappointment

I love you; I do
I love everything about you
Your beautiful mind, Your smile, Your laugh
Your dreams, Your sarcastic words
Your crazy facial expressions, Your heart
Your soul. . . I could go on and on

I especially love that lost little boy desperately trying to find
himself in this crazy world

Robin J.

I could clearly see
There was no future
For you and me
We were on two different levels in life

You, not ready to let go
Of everything that binds you to your past
Continually holding on to things
You should have released in life long ago
But who am I to tell you when to let go of it
And me, dealing with the same sh@t
Though eagerly wanting heal my broke pieces
Desperately attempting to untangle the past to be free
Trying to progress forward in life and love
Seems it is causing us both nothing but pain and misery
Our end goal was to be happy, in love together I thought or
maybe it was to simply be happy

Seems it just is not working out that way
It was best I leave
It was best you be self-governing
It was so much easier to have you let go of me
I sabotaged our ending to allow you to set US free

WORD PROMPT!

Disrespectful — *to show no respect in the way you speak or behave to someone*

I could have stayed, but why?
You showed me
In everything you said and did
That I was not the one
That I was not what you desired
Your tone of annoyance
The betrayal in your actions
There was nothing but disgust in your eyes
I would walk away as tears rolled down my face
I felt as though you never cared
That all the years we shared
Present but not present
I would have rather just been alone
Because of your **disrespectful** ways
It's why I chose not to stay

Robin J.

Your turn! Use the word *disrespect* in a poem...

_____

_____

_____

_____

_____

_____

_____

_____

_____

_____

_____

_____

_____

_____

_____

_____

I was simply a fool
Allowing you in
I let down my walls
Trusted you
Called you a friend

I knew, though
I should have been cautious from the start

It was games you were still playing
All at my expense

Should have known
You had not changed

Your name is still the same
Same smile
Same swag
Just your tone is what changed

I could kick myself
For trusting you

For allowing you to reside
In a place I never allow anyone

But I trusted you
Hoped you would change
I was such a fool

Robin J.

I often thought of
What it would be like if
We were to entwine our lives
In the beginning, it starts off passionate and fulfilling
In the middle, it begins to fade
In the end, we realized there is a definite passion between
us
But not enough to sustain the test of time
Along came all the bumpy roller coaster rides
Eventually, the passion died
I often wonder if we could have
Made this something beautiful
If we had entwined our lives

THE BREAKUP

So, I guess this is the breakup
But isn't this what you wanted?
I gave you years of my life
And you never did right
I put my trust in you, in us
I poured myself into your mold
Of what you wanted me to be
Needed me to be

At every turn you made this about you
You made me feel
I was never really what you ever wanted
It was about you from the beginning
It was never about me or us, not even remotely

I was inundated with you and this relationship
You always wanting more
Leaving little time for myself
Not even knowing me anymore
I was always accepting of what little
You brought to the table

So, I guess this is the breakup
I waited around as you served me nothing but scraps of
yourself
Never made me a priority, never heard my cries
And you definitely did not hear my goodbye
We could have been so good together forever

Robin J.

So I thought

I think from the start, I was never your first choice
Did you settle? Did I do the same?
Did we only waste each other's time?
Was this all in vain?

But you... With all your insecurities
All your selfish ways
Never taking time
To look at it from ny point of view
You could never see that, I loved only you

So, yeah, I guess this is the breakup
"You just don't love me how I want to be loved"
Is what I always heard from you
What about me? and how I needed to be loved

So, yes, this is the breakup

Breaking up from your
Selfishness
Your insecurities
Your self-centeredness
Your controlling ways
Your always having things your way
Yes, this is the breakup!

Just a Thought. . .

"If you keep riding the fence with people in your life, it becomes weak, broken in places, boards missing, and sometimes it just falls down completely. Do not be surprised if they do not take the time to repair it from you riding it. There is no riding the fence in life. You do, or you don't. You will, or you won't. You can, or you can't."

Robin J.

I AM are two powerful words! If you do not truly know who you are, how do you expect anyone else to know?

I AM Confident
I AM Beautiful
I AM Courageous
I AM Loved
I AM Stubborn
I AM Caring
I AM Peace
I AM Worthy
I AM Blessed
I AM Grateful
I AM Voiceful
I AM Thankful
I AM Prayerful

I AM excited about what each new day brings and excited I woke up to enjoy it.

Knowing who you are is so important in your journey of life, all the good stuff and bad sh@t. If you know who you are, no one can ever tell you anything about you that you do not already know to be true. Never forget your "I AM's" and always remember you are ENOUGH.

I AM . . . *(circle all that apply!)*

CARING	**SELFISH**	**GENEROUS**
TRUSTING	JUDGEMENTAL	BEAUTIFUL
STUBBORN	**COURAGEOUS**	**CONFIDENT**
SHY	FRIENDLY	QUIET
PATIENT	**AGGRESSIVE**	**SELFLESS**
CONSIDERATE	AFFECTIONATE	FORGIVING
RESOURCEFUL	**CONSISTENT**	**UNRELIABLE**
EMOTIONAL	MOODY	LOVING
IMPATIENT	**OPTIMISTIC**	**CREATIVE**
HARDWORKING	HONEST	HANDSOME
DECEPTIVE	**SARCASTIC**	**LOYAL**
REALISTIC	DRAMATIC	RESPONSIBLE
SELFLESS	**SELF-CRITICAL**	**HELPFUL**
COMPLEX	RESERVED	INDECISIVE
DEPENDABLE	**VOICEFUL**	**SUPPORTIVE**

Robin J.

Thoughts of you fill my days
Wondering
How you are and if you are okay
Just really want to call
To say hey! And Catch up
Reminisce about the good old days

Heard you have a girl now
Saw the pictures you took by your mom's house
The other day
You look happy and I hope you truly are

She is pretty
I hope y'all go far

Not much going on with me
Trying my best to forget you
And move on with my life
I miss you and wonder if you miss me, too

When I had my chance
I threw it all up in the air
Took you for granted
Made you feel less than a man
Now I am sitting here with my face in my hands
Wishing you were still mine
Oh, if we could turn back the hands of time
I would do it differently this time

I could not stay
Where there was no love

I could not pretend
We were happy in love

Up to my neck with your lies
I swear I was gonna drown

Walking away
Felt better than if I stayed

Please tell her
I wish you all well

I hope she knows
I am sure she does

She got a playa for life
I swear

I want nothing but the best for you
I hope you feel the same

Nothing last forever
So, we will just chalk this up to the game!

Robin J.

Empty words
Broken promises
Baby I love you's
Followed by
Years of tears
Permanent streaks
Down my face
I have somehow gotten to a sunken place
Someone please throw me some rope
Allow me to pull myself up
Mad at nobody but myself
For falling for your charm
Heard all the alarms
Ignoring them all
Hoping you would prove
Me out to be wrong
All I can do is
Shake my head and sigh
I knew from the beginning
You were just not right
Now I'm sitting here teary-eyed

I wanted his attention
And then I wanted
The love, the big house, the two kids
And the white picket fence
So, I did everything in my power to get it
Even though I knew in my heart
Right, he was not; he never would be
He showed me from the start
Maybe I was naive, or maybe I just didn't want to see it
I still bought into the dream he sold me
I believed I could change him
I believed my love was enough to mold him
Into all the things I wanted and needed him to be
In the end, it was not enough
Change starts with self
He had to want it for himself
Only he could change his ways
Nothing I could have ever done or said
Would mold him into something he was not
Had it not been for me learning my significance in this
world
I would have stayed and allowed the same toxic cycle to
continue
I thought I was happy. . .
At least, I thought that was what happiness was supposed
to look like, feel like, and sound like
I ignored all the signs
I covered the scars with smiles
Pretended we were happy during social gatherings
Prayed he could learn to love me genuinely
That all my time and energy was not in vain
That I would get a return on my 20-year investment

Robin J.

I was not happy, though
Walking around on eggshells
It all was still just a continuous repetition of our past
I yearned for something from him that I would never
receive
He was everything I dreamed of
And everything that frightened me

I am just a lost soul
Searching for a place that feels like home
Wanting my soul to be at peace
Searching for someone
Anyone who could absolutely just love me
Seems like the world has forgotten me
Left me to fend for myself
Living whichever way the wind blows
Just need some place to call home
Some place I can be free to be imperfectly me
Home is what my soul longs for
A place I can kick my feet up
A place where my soul can rest easy
Beneath an old willow tree

Robin J.

WORD PROMPT!

Absence — *state of being away or not being present*

I was torn between leaving and staying
Did not think it would matter either way
Your pre-occupation lately has gotten the best of you
You don't see it, but I do
We are in the same room but your **absence**
Breaks my heart
Tears me apart
I ask myself why I stay
When my **absence** would not matter to you anyway

Your turn! Use the word *absence* in a poem...

_____

_____

_____

_____

_____

_____

_____

I remember every time, every line
The way your voice sounded in my ear
As you made love to me from behind
As you whispered sweet untruths
Like a dove's coo in the morning dew
I remember every touch, every rub
The way your hands felt going down my back
As they grabbed my hips and pulled me close
The way your lips brushed my face
As I looked into your eyes
And you repeated lie after lie
I remember every scent
Every edge of your frame
How your eyes sparkled when I would say your name
How your lips trembled before you would lie
And how you never could quite look me in my eyes
How I remember you oh so well
And all the lies you use to tell

Robin J.

When I saw you for the first time in over 30 years
I could not help but stare
I got butterflies
I felt like a high school girl with a crush all over again
I admit my nerves got the best of me
But there you were after all these years
Just as handsome as you were as a young man
I did not know what to say
Or even if words would form to come out of my mouth
If we happened to cross paths

All those old feelings came flooding back
Those old high school crush feelings, the feeling of lust
Feelings of "I cannot live without you"

I remember how you made me laugh
All the silly fun times we shared
I remember how you used to bite my cheeks
How you would bear hug me, smack my butt, and it would
make me weak
I can still hear you whisper in my ear how much you loved
me
How we would lay for hours talking about all our dreams
How you wanted forever with me and me with you

I wanted so badly to walk over and say, "Hi, or Hello, and
ask How have you been?"
I was frozen, unable to move, just staring at you from across
the room

You looked my way and smiled
I remember that smile all too well

A ball of nerves, hands shaking
You walked across the room, right in my direction
I looked up to greet you, but you walked right past
As if I was not even standing there
I turned to see where you went
I see you hugging someone
She's PRETTY
I felt empty and couldn't help but stare

How could you not remember me
Five long years I gave you
How could you just pass me by
You did not even look my way or bat an eye
I smelled you as you passed; you still smell the same

How I wish she were me
Someone you were happy to see
How could you forget me and all we were meant to be
I am doubting now if you even cared
I could not help but stare

Robin J.

WRITE AN ACROSTIC POEM

A poem in which the first letter of each line spells out a word, name, or phrase when read vertically.

Poems written
On paper
Each word
Meticulously placed

Your turn. Write an acrostic poem of your own...

_____

_____

_____

_____

_____

_____

_____

_____

Tell me I am wrong
For wanting you to love me the way I love you
Am I wrong for needing you to need me the way I need you
Am I wrong for expecting you to keep your word the way I
keep mine
Am I wrong for accepting you for who you are
All your flaws and rough edges
And expecting you to do the same
Am I wrong for wanting your eyes only for me
Cause for me, you are all I see
Am I wrong for trusting you to do right
Am I wrong for wanting us to have the American Dream
Am I wrong for wanting you to give your best
Am I wrong for putting your love to the test
Am I wrong for wanting you to just be my King
Am I wrong for seeing in you what no one else sees
And wanting you to see that in me
Am I wrong for giving you 100% of me
When I do not even give that to myself
Am I wrong for wanting to be your beacon
So that you can see the light
Am I wrong for standing by you
Through the pain
WHEN I HAVE NOTHING TO GAIN
Tell me, am I wrong?
For just wanting you to do the same

Robin J.

Ain't no sunshine
When he is home
Walking around on pins and needles
Holding my breath for fear of breathing too loud
Never knowing when he will strike out
Even trying to whisper quietly to my soul

Sometimes we cannot see how beautiful people are because of all the scars they have not allowed to heal.

Robin J.

ONE-SIDED

My vision is one-sided
I can see all the things
That were meant to be between you and me
Though I cannot see the agony that I have caused you

Something in me
Cannot comprehend that you are right and I am wrong
I can only comprehend that you should just be grateful
That I am still here

My vision is so one-sided
I do not see your daily struggles
Your daily tears
The damage and daily distress
Caused by me
I only see all you should be thankful for
And all I bring to the table, even though there is no table for
you to sit at and nothing for you to eat, eat on, eat with or
drink

My vision is so one-sided
I do not understand why you cry, why you fuss, and
scream
I do not see all the reasons I give you to be so mean
I do not realize how my words come off mean
All I see is you constantly nagging me

I do not hear you when you cry
When you beg for me to try
I do not realize that I am the one f@cking this dream up

My vision is so one-sided
I cannot see all that you have to offer me
I cannot see all your beauty or all my complexities
Because my vision is so one-sided
All I can ever see is me
My vision is so one-sided

Robin J.

His voice was intoxicating.
  The intelligence flowing out of his full, perfect lips
      was exhilarating.

To have a deep, thought-provoking exchange of words
    was refreshing.
      He is a man with something to say.

A man with substance and grace,
    he challenges his self every day
        to be a better version of himself than yesterday.

He is confident, and it shows in everything he does and
everything he says.
    It oozes from his pores.
      It reflects in his smile.

If you ever have the pleasure of his embrace,
    it captures you and leaves you craving for more of him.

Yes, he is intoxicating with intelligence flowing from him
onto those with the opportunity to be in his presence,
    feel his essence,
        and partake in his intelligence.

Damn near perfection this man is.
    If you see him, you will know exactly who he is.

It is okay to let go now . . . You can do it.
You've been holding on to all of that sh@t for too long.
Let it go and allow yourself to be free!

Let go of past heartbreaks. . . Your heart was broken for a reason. . . It showed you how to love.

Let go of people who have hurt you or wronged you in the past. . . You were hurt or wronged for a reason. . . It showed you to be mindful of who you allow in your circle.

Let go of situations from your past. . . Those situations happened for a reason. . . It showed you how to be a better person.

Let go of sh@t. You have no control of people you have no control over. Situations you have no control over, let it go!

Today, I let go of...

_____

_____

_____

_____

_____

Learn from it, embrace it, grow through it, and let that sh@t go!

Robin J.

You post her
Yet you run to me
Every opportunity you get
Yet
You post
You're happy
In love with her
You cry on my phone
Cause she left you home alone
But then you post
That you're happy
In love with her
You express your unhappiness
How she doesn't let you be your best
You tell me I am the one for you
Without me, what would you do?
But then you post
That you're happy
In love with her
You complain she doesn't support your dreams
Doesn't allow you to be king
But then you post
That you're happy
In love with her

It has been 24 hours and counting
Since I last texted you
I am holding on to my boundaries
I have now set for you
You did not appreciate
My presence in your world
Took me for granted. . .HA
Thought I would always be there. . .HA
Fooled you
Have I wanted to text you. . .YEAH!
I thought of all kinds of things to say about
What has been happening throughout my day
I wanted so badly to share, but you wouldn't care
So, these boundaries
I have set are to benefit ME
They are to keep me in check
With my feelings and actions
And as for you, they are to annoy you
Because you don't know they are there
You just see I am acting weird and like I don't care
Love should not be so complex
Relationships should not be so unaccommodating
It has been 24 hours since I last texted you
I promised myself if you text, I would not respond
If you call, I will not answer the phone

Ring, ring, ring. . . Hello! Guess I lied to myself

Robin J.

The minute I start acting like you
There seems to be a problem
You stay with an attitude

When I don't answer your calls
Or ignore your text
You always accuse me
Of being with my ex

When we're together and my mind
Is not all there
You always accuse me that I do not care

When I am rarely available to spend time with you
And do the things you want to do
You constantly accuse me of being untrue

When I get dressed up in my "f@ck'em" dress
Step out at night to release some stress
You always accuse me of being a hoe
But little do you know
And what you cannot even see
Is everything you accuse me of
Are all the things you've done to me

WORD PROMPT!

Counterproposal — *a proposal offered as an alternative to a previous proposal.*

He came to me with that smug look and that sly smile
Telling me everything I wanted to hear
How much he loved me and would treat me right
How I am the most beautiful woman in the world and how
he could make me feel
How he would give me all his time
That he would be my king and I would be his queen
He would give me the world
I have seen his type before, and I almost fell for him
I smiled back with a smug look and sly smile
Told him, "Do not make promises you cannot keep"
We do not want to get caught up in a situationship
I am not wanting this to get too deep
Not looking for love, let us just keep this simple
No catching feelings, no having to spend time, no cuddling
No pressure to call or text
Or me coming to your place or you coming to mine
Just hit my phone whenever you have the time
We can do what it does and just keep this at just a f@ck
That way, no one gets stuck
The look on his face, I could not help but smile
Just keeping it real with him
Nothing more, nothing less
I could tell he did not like my **counterproposal**

Robin J.

Your turn! Use the word *counterproposal* in a poem...

_____

_____

_____

_____

_____

_____

_____

_____

_____

_____

_____

_____

_____

_____

She acts like Spring
Talks like Summer
And
Walks
Like
Thunder

Robin J.

The games you play
You play them well

You are the king of dodgeball
And play hide and seek with the skills of a magician
If hopscotch had a title, you would be champion

I see those silly little games you play
And though you play them well
Naive I am not

I let you play
Letting you think
Things are going your way

Something you never knew
I play games, too, just like you do!

Sometimes, you must let go and let it be
Some things just are not meant for you
Seems the more you hold on to it
It starts to turn blue from a lack of blood flow
Then, eventually, it turns black
And because you couldn't let go
It falls off from a lack of blood flow
Or it must be amputated because you still are not willing to
let go
If only at the beginning of it all
You stopped and realized that
It was changing color, turning pale and blue
Then maybe you would have allowed it too just be
And let it go, setting you and it free
Maybe you would have allowed life to flow through it
And not applied more pressure
In the end
It died slowly
And painfully
When it did not have to
If you could have just let it go
Instead of holding on

Robin J.

WORD PROMPT!

Profoundness — *the property of being very deep, without limit.*

I want you to look at ME
And truly see ME
All the layers of ME
Not just the surface of my skin

But the **profoundness** of my being
To see all my flaws
All my merits

I want you to want more from me
Than being in between my sheets and legs
Hearing me moan your name

Can you see all I have to offer?
Will you be unflinching
To see the factual me

To look past the shell
And see the actual me
I want you to look at me
And love all of me
Not just the surface you can see

Your turn! Use the word *profoundness* in a poem...

_____

_____

_____

_____

_____

_____

_____

_____

_____

_____

_____

_____

_____

_____

_____

_____

Robin J.

Just a Thought. . .

I wonder when we are going to truly know our worth
When will we stop buying into what society tells us
we should and should not be?
When will we stop settling for crazy situationships and
bullsh@t?
When will we heal OUR
Broken men
Broken women
Broken children
Broken homes
When will we see that we are worth way more
Then all the bulls@t we settle for
When will we stand up and say NO MORE
And adorn our heads with those crowns once more

Dear Ex,

I want to Thank You
I want to thank you for making me the woman I am today
Thank you for showing what a man is not supposed to be
Thank you for showing me what love is not supposed to be
Thank you for showing me how a marriage is not supposed
to work
Thank you for not ever putting me first
Thank you for making it all about you
Thank you for never loving me the way a husband should
Thank you for wasting years of my life
Thank you for showing me all these things
Because of you
I now know what a man is supposed to be
I now know what love truly is
I now know how a marriage is supposed to work
I now know to put myself first
I now know it is about me, too
I now know loving you just made me a fool
I now know my time is precious and not to be wasted
I now know my self-worth was the lesson
And that I am worth more than you could ever afford
Thank you for making me the woman I am today

Robin J.

WORD PROMPT!

Talebearer — *a person who maliciously gossips or reveals secrets.*

I trusted her with all my life
Even let her have a key to the crib
Told her how my man put it down in bed
And all my secrets I held within
To only find out in the end
That she was a low-down, dirty, no-good **talebearer**
And damn sure was not my friend.

Your turn! Use the word *talebearer* in a poem…

_____

_____

_____

_____

_____

_____

_____

Let me
Ride your mind
Up and down
Each stroke
Slow and deliberate

With every word
My body trembles
From the thought
Of
Soft caresses
And
Kisses covering
Every inch of me

Laying for hours
Engulfed in each syllable of your intellect
Our bodies entwined
Bracing myself for penetration

Of every word spoken from your soft lips
Wet from the sound of the nouns
Floating out of your mouth
Like that first lick
When it has been a while
Captivated by how you articulate your thoughts

I love riding your beautiful mind
Slow so I can catch each vowel with every stroke
And each stroke more intense

Robin J.

Then the last
Let me ride your mind
I promise to take my time

Magnetic he is
He speaks with a confident tongue
Uses words as foreplay
In hopes of getting you sprung
Seductive in his speech
He is sure to leave you wanting more

He is emotionally unavailable
Though he is always at your beck and call
Readily ready with his charm
That always leaves you wanting more

Oh, how I adore him
When he saunters through that door
Chocolate oozing out the foundation
Of God's masterful creation

He is a man of intrigue
A man of intellect
If you are not careful
You will fall for him every time
He will pull you in with that handsome grin
Only to leave you empty inside

In one full sweep, he will have you
Enthralled in his presence
With his magnetic ways

Magnetic he is
He will capture your heart

Robin J.

Only to leave you down on your knees
With waterfalls pouring from your eyes
Asking yourself over and over, "Why me?"

You ever meet someone that just takes your breath away
They say all the right things, do all the right things
They are kind, considerate, loving, attentive, consistent
Everything you need, everything you want
They get you when no one else does
They make you feel everything you should be, everything
you could be
They believe in you when you don't believe in yourself
Everything about them speaks life into you

But you…

Find every reason why it shouldn't work
Why it couldn't work
You safeguard your heart
Because deep down you know
They could be the one
You could give your heart away to

You convince yourself
That something must be wrong
You want to open up and let them in
But you are terrified of it not working
You are scared of rejection
Being hurt all over again

So, you convince yourself that this person is not for you
You look for all their imperfections
You fight against someone that could be so right
For you on so many levels

Robin J.

You allow your own fears and insecurities to get in the way
Of someone who could possibly love you
In all the right ways

Two imperfect people
living in
their own
imperfect world
loving each other perfectly imperfect
but happy in their imperfections
living life their way
just loving on each other
despite themselves at times
and care not what the world has to say

Robin J.

Let us just keep this as a f@ck
Don't want to get our emotions involved
I just want some d@ck when I want it
Let me slide this wet p@ssy down on it
So, answer when I call
I promise it won't take long
Not trying to take all your time
Just want a little bump and grind
No need in catchin' feelings
I am leaving them under lock and key
No, I don't want to cuddle afterwards
Just wash up, get dressed, and walk yo' a$$ out the door
The world has made me this way
Coldhearted and emotionless
Not wanting to give my love away
To just anyone that passes my way
Got my middle finger up, screamin', "F@CK LOVE"
So, let us just keep this as a f@ck
No need for deep conversations
I just need some well rhythmed penetration
No back rubs, no lingering stares
Can you just pass me my panties
So, I can get the f@ck out of here
And, no I don't want a hug
Allow me to retreat
Back to my safe place
With my heart under lock and key
Remember, I did not bring my heart
Did you forget that part
I know I told you that from the start
Don't want to make this complicated
Do not want this to end up in disarray

With our hearts left cracked on the floor
And one of us leaving, slamming the door
Shhh! Just f@ck me; let your d@ck do what it does best
No conversation needed
There is no reason for you to know anything more about me
Is this some type of test?
Isn't all p@ssy the same?
So, let's just continue to play this game
So neither one of us gets caught up
Let us charge it to the game!
Got my middle finger up, Screamin', "F@ck love"
Let us just keep this as a f@ck
Shhh! Let's just f@ck

Robin J.

I refuse to settle for a piece of a man
Just to have a piece of a man
For I would not give him just a piece of me
I refuse to listen to your foolish lies
Any pieces of your lies
Lies that would never come from me
I am not settling for just a piece of a man
With foolish lies
Doing nothing more than trying to take advantage of me

I hope you utterly understand
That I think more of myself
Than to believe your foolishness
I see through all those lies
Especially when I look into those deceitful eyes
Than to just settle for pieces of you
Because I do not give you just pieces of me

I just need you to be THE Man
And not just a man that spits foolish lies
And only gives pieces of himself
That is not what I want, nor do I desire
Just pieces of a foolish man who spits nothing but foolish lies
Cause I would never give him just pieces of me

A ball of confusion,
With nothing but constant delusions
In the dark, shadows peers out
A whirlwind of chaos that constantly flows
My mind hears chaos that echoes wherever I go
In a world where everyone is insane
Where disorganization is the game
How do you contain
Constant chaos in your brain
How do you refrain
From not going insane
And becoming a part of the mental game

The screaming, the constant yelling in my brain
The voices from hell
Makes it sometimes hard to maintain
Confusion makes me weak
Often losing sleep,
As the chaos continues to creep

It fills my days, haunts my nights
It is all around me , seems there is no light in sight
I cannot escape it
Trying hard not to partake in it
Darkness abounds as I constantly fight for a peaceful sound
Chaos speaks as it causes me to remain weak
A constant
Wondering if this is a nightmare
And when will I wake up out of my sleep
Or will this chaos forever I will keep

Robin J.

WRITE A HAIKU POEM USING
THE WORD "REVERENCE"

A haiku poem is composed of only 3 lines. The first line of the haiku has 5 syllables, the second line has 7 syllables, and the third has 5 syllables.

She watched in **reverence**
As he strolled across the stage
Astonished was she

Your turn. Write a haiku poem of your own...

_____

_____

_____

_____

_____

_____

_____

It was beautiful
Until it wasn't
We complemented each other in so many ways
Funny, though, how when life goes on, things change
I cooked, and he cleaned the dishes
I washed clothes, and he folded them
I put them up, and he ironed
He mowed the lawn, and I trimmed the bushes

He rapped, and I sang
He drove, and I slept comfortably in the passenger seat
I pushed the bar, and he chilled
I stressed, and he remained at peace
He spoke life into me, and I received it

It was beautiful
Until it wasn't
Funny how we take small things for granted
Funny how we complement each other without even
knowing
Funny how we do not get it until it's gone
It was everything I ever needed and wanted
It was beautiful until it wasn't

Robin J.

If no one has told you lately,
you are doing a great job.
Keep that sh@t up!

About the Author

Robin J. is a first-time author and has been a lifelong writer of poetry. She first began writing and learning different poetry styles in the fourth grade. Robin considers herself an Urban Poet and writes about everyday life experiences in her poetry.

Robin grew up in Wichita, Kansas, but also lived in New Orleans, Louisiana. She currently resides in Dallas, Texas, and is the mother of seven adult children. Finally, she has made time to work on her poetry books to share with others.

Have a message for Robin J.?

She welcomes you to reach out to her by email at PoetryForTheSoul@yahoo.com.